MW00390248

hello@thenelsonproject.org
www.thenelsonproject.org
Austin, TX

ISBN 978-0-692-16275-0

Disclaimer: This workbook is not intended as financial, legal, or broker advice. Regulations, standards, license requirements, and license ethics may vary in your area, region, state, or brokerage. Licensed REALTORS® must consult their broker for legal, client and contract advice. Unlicensed (pre-license) folks cannot give the impression that they may be licensed and, thus, cannot take the majority of actions outlined in this book. Acting like a licensed real estate agent when you are not licensed is illegal. Know the rules in your state, learn the nuances in your area. The author does not take any responsibility for the results of your actions as prescribed in this book. This publication is not affiliated with any particular real estate broker, brokerage, or franchise.

The author is legally and ethically bound by the standards and ethics of the NATIONAL ASSOCIATION OF REALTORS® and the Texas Real Estate Commission, and personally bound by the golden rule. The author, Julie Nelson, is a licensed REALTOR® in the State of Texas.

This Success Faster workbook and the Success Faster book (Success Faster: Quickly Launch or Relaunch Your Real Estate Career (your roadmap to getting started or starting over), and subsequent publications or products distributed or sold are in no way affiliated with any particular real estate broker, brokerage, or franchise. All information within these pages is the creation of Julie Nelson and The Nelson Project Inc.

ABOUT THE AUTHOR

Julie Nelson and The Nelson Project Inc. created this guide to help REALTORS® and other entrepreneurs succeed. Business strategist, career advisor, speaker, trainer, coach, problem solver, path finder, and general enthusiast, Julie Nelson is a nearly twenty-year veteran of the real estate industry including a five-year assignment running one of the largest new agent broker training programs in the country. Julie is an active Realtor in Austin, Texas. thenelsonproject.com is Julie's real estate business, thenelsonproject.org is Julie's training, coaching and entrepreneurial blog. Julie lives on her somewhat urban farm in Austin, Texas. When not doing real estate stuff, you will find Julie in her gardens or on her bike.

Improve the trajectory, and overall enjoyment, of your business and your life, and you will change your world. Period. Change your world and you will set things in motion that inevitably will change another life. Divine. I believe we are all on this planet to participate in this process. My sacred mission is to help you do that.

OUTLINE

INTRODUCTION & ROADMAP

FOUNDATION

1. Key Ingredients
2. My Last 10 Clients
3. My Accountability Partners
4. My Success Vision (book reference Chapters 1, 5)
5. My Performance Review (book reference Chapter 7)
6. My Power Score (book reference Chapter 8)

ACTION INGREDIENTS

1. Clients Quickly (book reference Chapter 6)
2. The Double Down Exercise
3. Flex-time vs Full-time vs Part-time (book reference Chapter 5)
4. A Cash Exercise (book reference Chapter 16)
5. The Revenue Lifecycle And The Role Of Referrals (book reference Chapters 6, 16)
6. My Business Goals … A Simple Math Exercise (book reference Chapter 16)
7. Conversations (book reference Chapter 9)
8. The Power Questions (book reference Chapter 10)
9. My People (book reference Chapter 12)
10. My Online Audit (book reference Chapter 13)
11. My Action Plan
12. Action Items & Script Reference (book reference: back reference sections)
13. My Vision
14. Book Club Group Discussion Guide

INTRODUCTION & ROADMAP

What you think matters. What you do matters more
(because it will affect what you think ...funny how that works).

This workbook is designed as a tool, study guide, action plan, and mastermind guide to accommodate the book Success Faster: Quickly Launch or Relaunch Your Real Estate Career (your roadmap to getting started or starting over), by Julie Nelson. You may be taking this class in your local board, or you may have purchased this online as your own workbook and study guide.

With a vision of helping more agents succeed, stabilize their businesses, correct their work/life balance, get to the next level, and reconnect to the joy factor, the Success Faster book was published by Julie Nelson on Amazon in early 2018. Very quickly, it became clear that the Realtor audience was not only responding to the fresh perspective and usefulness of the roadmap, the reader wanted more. Will you help me? Can you make the book into a class? Will you come speak to our group? Where were you when I was just getting started?

This workbook will serve as a tool, a roadmap for …

Brand new agents in search of cash flow and a success roadmap.

Relaunching agents in search of balance, stability, and a roadmap to do it better this time around.

Established agents seeking a course correction, fresh tools, a healthier pipeline and work/life balance.

Teams in need of a practical tool to ramp up or re-ramp the sales team.

Brokers in search of an effective and relatable tool to help their new, emerging, and middle producers.

Mastermind groups and book clubs looking for engaging dialogue, practical tools and scripts.

This workbook is a roadmap for many.

Your results with this material will depend on your efforts, your accountability, how you are showing up, and your ability to take action. Your results with this material will depend even more on your ability to circle back around and do the actions again and again and again. And then again and again and again. This cycle of taking action is not necessarily sexy but it is the work, the job, the ongoing effort of how to gain momentum and stability in your business. The work and job are not necessarily the sexy part … the momentum, the related cash flow, the efficiencies, the happy clients, the changed lives, the improved vacations … that's what we want, right? We call this net happiness and that is where we are going.

Your Accounting 101 class taught you about net income and net profit. (I sure wish real estate schools & licensing would cover some of these business basics. Sigh.) I believe the true bottom line is net happiness. Net happiness is when you experience the results of your work, the results of your repetitive action of consistently getting the most important things done every day. Net happiness is when your business and your life are working at a higher, self-actualized level. It's holistic business.

This workbook is designed to help you get into a consistent mode and pattern where you are getting the important things done every day. Not the shiny objects and the 100 administrative things you need to do, but the most important things … done … first … every day. Don't get me wrong, I can chase shiny objects with the best shiny object chasers out there and my desk is full of tasks awaiting my attention! The trick is simply progress on the most important things, nothing else! I know, this is so basic but, honestly, getting the right things done is the big differentiator between nailing it and falling short or feeling behind. It's why I, we, you need a roadmap, course corrections, and then more course corrections, and why you may need a coach or at least some accountability partners in place to master the skill, craft, and art of forward progress.

This workbook is both a summary and an expansion of the action items and scripts outlined in the Success Faster book.

Let's get started.

FOUNDATION #1: KEY INGREDIENTS

If we were to outline the full roadmap to success, it would involve pages and pages, and the class would last for days, perhaps weeks. This success formula applies to both a launch (new agents) or a relaunch (not new agents). The success formula is key to gaining clients and momentum now. Everything changes in this business, including your psyche and your bank account, once you have a healthy lineup of clients and leads and contracts and paychecks. So our focus throughout the workbook is on building leads and momentum and cash flow NOW. How to deal with those leads and momentum and cash flow is another class. Let's take a closer look.

The Success Formula, Key Ingredients:

Action

Clients

Lead Pipeline

Database

Cashflow

The Power Ingredient: Your Last 10 Clients

First, we are going to run through some fundamentals that we will reference off and on. Each of these fundamentals has a task outlined in the next few pages and these tasks / exercises will serve as the foundation for the rest of the workbook. Once we cover the six foundational pieces, then we will dig in to action ingredients that are designed to move you forward quickly and simply. We will NOT over-complicate this business … prepare to keep it simple! Keep this goal in mind: you gaining traction and clients quickly. Let's jump in!

FOUNDATION #2: MY LAST 10 CLIENTS

Your next paycheck is closer than you think.

Let's jump right in with the first hands-on activity of the workbook. We will reference this throughout the class / workbook. If you are a new agent, then your homework is to ask this question (like, today … pick up the phone right now or post something on Facebook asking your Realtor network the source of their last 10 clients) … examples are sphere, past client referral, open house, internet lead, FSBO, friend, bff, friend of friend, family, family referral, former colleague. For not new agents, quickly write down the name and source of your last ten clients (this exercise should only take a few minutes).

Here is the source of my last 10 clients or leads:

ONE.

TWO.

THREE.

FOUR.

FIVE.

SIX.

SEVEN.

EIGHT.

NINE.

TEN.

We will reference this list throughout the workbook. Remember this construct: Your next paycheck is closer than you think … and it has a lot to do with this list.

FOUNDATION #3:
MY ACCOUNTABILITY PARTNERS

It's not like you have a boss who is checking in on your progress every day or every week. Who is the boss of you?

There is a ton of research on this topic. Let's just agree that you have a greater likelihood of significant progress when you attach some accountability. So this is one of our foundational pieces. Let's set up your accountability team by completing the following (yes, you can change this later):

PARTNER ONE. One personal person I will tell about my goals and schedule and intentions is (this may be a significant other, bff, trusted advisor):

PARTNER TWO. One professional colleague I will tell about my goals and schedule and intentions is

MASTERMIND. My mastermind group looks like this:

FOUNDATION #4: MY SUCCESS VISION

You can only become truly accomplished at something you love. Don't make money your goal. Instead, pursue the things you love doing, and then do them so well that people can't take their eyes off you.
– Maya Angelou

What is your vision, your goal, your dream? Where do you want to be in one year? or five? Take a few minutes and attach some words to your vision.

ONE. My success vision … when I hit my goals, it is going to look and feel something like this:

TWO. One thing I want to create in my life is

THREE. What I love most about my business is … or the reasons I got into this business in the first place are

---

FOUNDATION #5: MY PERFORMANCE REVIEW

The good news? You are your own boss. The bad news? You are your own boss. Don't be a lousy one.

My Performance Review

Am I being a good boss? Let's take a closer look:

Bossy Things	Rating 1(low) ....10 (high)									
I have sales goals & I track them.	1	2	3	4	5	6	7	8	9	10
I get the most important things done every day.	1	2	3	4	5	6	7	8	9	10
I have minimized distractions.	1	2	3	4	5	6	7	8	9	10
I maintain a full time schedule.	1	2	3	4	5	6	7	8	9	10
I am busy with the right things.	1	2	3	4	5	6	7	8	9	10
I show up on time.	1	2	3	4	5	6	7	8	9	10
My work/life balance is in check.	1	2	3	4	5	6	7	8	9	10
I rarely get distracted by social media.	1	2	3	4	5	6	7	8	9	10
I have tools in place to track my pipeline & reference them often.	1	2	3	4	5	6	7	8	9	10
I add to my pipeline every week.	1	2	3	4	5	6	7	8	9	10
I get back on track quickly & easily.	1	2	3	4	5	6	7	8	9	10
I have leverage (help) in my business.	1	2	3	4	5	6	7	8	9	10
I have a monthly P&L.	1	2	3	4	5	6	7	8	9	10
I regularly review my financial statements.	1	2	3	4	5	6	7	8	9	10
My expenses are in check.	1	2	3	4	5	6	7	8	9	10
I do what I say I am going to do.	1	2	3	4	5	6	7	8	9	10
Would I hire me?	1	2	3	4	5	6	7	8	9	10

In reviewing the bossy things above, how am I doing overall? What overall score would I give myself?

What would make it better?

In reviewing the bossy things above,

- one thing I totally have down is

- one thing I would like to improve immediately is

- one thing I will focus on this month is

- one action I could take today to improve my score is

- one action I could take this week to improve my pipeline is

If I was a lousy boss this week, what got in my way?

What are three things I could have done differently?

My fastest route to a new lead, client or paycheck today is

FOUNDATION #6: MY POWER SCORE

How you show up matters.

Power score is that somewhat intangible, yet moderately palpable thing that combines your energy, your confidence, your eye contact, your voice, your posture, your motivation, your nutrition, your internal dialogue…simply, how you're showing up in the world. Power score can be situational. Power score is not an introvert / extrovert thing. This is an awareness exercise identifying how you tend to show up. Circle the items that resonate with you or tend to show up in your world.

POWER SCORE 1-3. THE LOW ZONE

- My confidence could be better.
- High energy is a bit elusive.
- Business phone calls tend to put a knot in my stomach.
- Often, I lack the energy to press forward or to feel excited about taking action.
- My immediate circle of friends (or family) leans negative and pessimistic and consistently attempts to sabotage my drive and optimism.
- Direct eye contact is not my strongest suit.
- My sleep, eating, exercise habits sort of suck.
- Optimism is a bit of a distant cousin.

POWER SCORE 4-6. THE MEDIUM ZONE

- I have some challenges (home, health, financial) that I have to work around.
- Sometimes (or too often) I have to muster up my energy.
- I am that nice and steady person of few words.
- I am the keen observer who is rarely the outspoken cheerleader but rather the reliable and consistent authority.
- I am almost never the loudest voice in the room.
- I am the steady team player everyone relies on to get things done.

POWER SCORE 7-10. THE HIGH ZONE

- I attract people.
- I raise my hand often.
- Most days, my energy is solid.
- I am a leader.
- I move quickly.
- I have Energizer Bunny tendencies.
- If I hit a bump, I keep moving forward.
- I am consistently positive and optimistic.
- Swagger comes easy.
- I have decent sleep, eating, and exercise habits.

POWER SCORE, PART 2

I consider myself more of an introvert … or an extrovert:

01 ← — 02 — 03 — 04 — 05 — 06 — 07 — 08 — 09 — 10 →

Introvert, social takes energy   Mid-range   Extrovert, social
& then I need recharge   gives me energy!

Overall, on most days, I believe my power score is in this range:

01 ← — 02 — 03 — 04 — 05 — 06 — 07 — 08 — 09 — 10 →

Low to lowish   Mid-range   High

Consistency: my power score is …

01 ← — 02 — 03 — 04 — 05 — 06 — 07 — 08 — 09 — 10 →

Inconsistent, it's all over the   It moves around a bit   Consistent, always
place.   the same

Power score agility: When I have a low power day, I can usually power through …

01 ← — 02 — 03 — 04 — 05 — 06 — 07 — 08 — 09 — 10 →

I may as well take the day off because   I have some agility around this.   I totally power through because
I'm totally non-productive in the low zone.   I have to get my job done.

When I have a low power score day, the culprit tends to be

```
┌─────────────────────────────────────────────┐
│                                             │
│                                             │
│                                             │
│                                             │
└─────────────────────────────────────────────┘
```

The things that help me stay in high power score mode are

```
┌─────────────────────────────────────────────┐
│                                             │
│                                             │
│                                             │
│                                             │
│                                             │
└─────────────────────────────────────────────┘
```

CLIENTS QUICKLY ... LET'S DIG IN

I fully understand that I am in the business of talking to people about real estate (and I act that way):

01 ← 02 — 03 — 04 — 05 — 06 — 07 — 08 — 09 — 10 →

I really need work on this.   Middle of the road.   I am consistently mailing this. A++

How hungry am I for my next 1, 3, 5, 10 paychecks? Is my motivation more financial or simply accomplishment or both?

Fast beats smart ... here is what that means to me:

What is my fastest route to a lead or client today?

Review your last 10 clients source list ... my main source or two is

The type of client I love the most is

One thing I am really good at in real estate is

One thing that is already working at a moderate to high level in my business is

Here are some free things I do that tend to generate business:

A phone call I could make right now is

DOUBLE DOWN EXERCISE

Now that we have reviewed what is already working in your business, what comes naturally to you, and what you like, let's take a closer look at how you can double down. The theory here is that you will get faster and easier results, more clients, greater conversion, more bank, and more enjoyment when you do more of what is already working. In poker, double down is a term that basically says that my hand is potentially pretty darn good so I am going to increase my bet. In business and in life, it means doing more of what you love or what comes easy. Remember, your next client may be closer than you think. Let's take a closer look.

MY WHEELHOUSE. My #1 source of leads or clients is (reference last 10 clients exercise, this is not a precise exercise, general percentages will do … where is my business currently coming from?)

DOUBLE DOWN. I can double-down on this by doing the following:

Here is a quick list of the people I have on speed dial or the favorites list on my phone:

```
┌─────────────────────────────────────────────────────────────────┐
│                                                                   │
│                                                                   │
│                                                                   │
│                                                                   │
│                                                                   │
│                                                                   │
└─────────────────────────────────────────────────────────────────┘
```

Here is the amount of business (leads, referrals, clients, direct business) I am getting from my speed dial group:

01 ← 02 — 03 — 04 — 05 — 06 — 07 — 08 — 09 — 10 →

None at all or barely.   Some, definitely room for improvement.   Crushing it with my speed dial group!

Here is the extent to which I have shared my vision and goals with my speed dial group (and other VIP's) and have directly asked for their referrals this year:

01 ← 02 — 03 — 04 — 05 — 06 — 07 — 08 — 09 — 10 →

Barely, if at all.   Some, definitely room for improvement.   All the time, super direct, unapologetic.

If open houses are a solid source for you, what are one or two things you can do to increase your results (examples: more of them, higher price point, improved follow-up, door-knock, social media push, improved signage)?

```
┌─────────────────────────────────────────────────────────────────┐
│                                                                   │
│                                                                   │
│                                                                   │
│                                                                   │
│                                                                   │
│                                                                   │
└─────────────────────────────────────────────────────────────────┘
```

With my top two sources of leads and clients, here is how much social media I put out related to those activities:

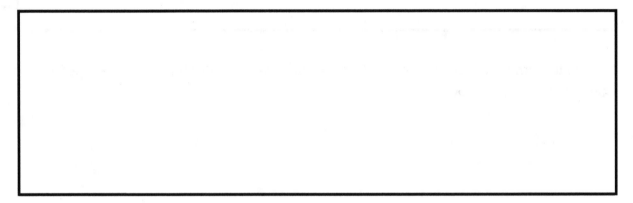

Here are a couple things I would like to explore or improve on social media:

Here is how I rate myself on lead follow-up:

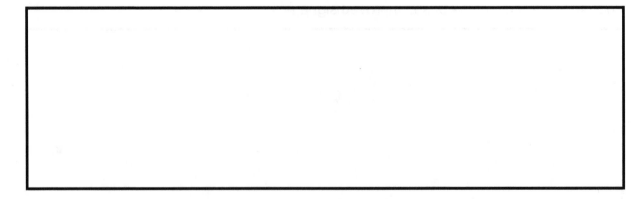

Here is something I can do to improve my follow-up:

FLEX-TIME VS FULL-TIME VS PART-TIME

There are many successful agents who started out part-time and there are many full-time agents with schedule limitations. And part of the appeal of your independent contractor status is the flex schedule, right? Let's work through an exercise to grasp the reality of your schedule and how to best work that into your success formula.

My non-negotiable schedule components / commitments look like this:

My typical work-week looks like this:

MON

TUES

WED

THURS

FRI

SAT

SUN

How many hours am I working in real estate per week?

How many hours do I spend on lead gen & lead follow-up?

I have days completely eaten up with admin & details vs I am super leveraged:

01 — 02 — 03 — 04 — 05 — 06 — 07 — 08 — 09 — 10

I regularly get buried in detail & admin.   Definitely room for improvement.   I spend very little time on detail & admin... I'll have systems & help.

I am very consistent with lead generation and lead follow-up … or am I?

01 — 02 — 03 — 04 — 05 — 06 — 07 — 08 — 09 — 10

Uh, no! Definitely needs work.   Middle of the road.   Super consistent! A++

Jumping-Off Point - You have a 42% greater chance of hitting your goal if you write it down. If you are part-time in real estate, write down when you will shift to full-time (pick one or both):

Full-time Target Date:

$$ in the Bank Target:

CASH!

Seriously, this could (should) be a stand-alone class, but let's make sure you understand the basics of your business finances. Due to the personal nature of this page, you may want to finish it out at home, but let's at least get started ...

First, a little questionnaire: true / false / other?

Budgeting is one of my super powers, I know my financial numbers:

I have a solid financial cushion:

I have clear & written financial goals:

I know where I stand right now in relation to my year goals:

I am on track:

At least every few months, II review every little expense in my business:

I am paying x for leads (like Zillow premium or other lead programs):

I know the ROI on the above expenditures:

I may be wasting money on the following:

My fastest route to a new client today is (yes, this is a repeat question):

```

```

My fixed business costs:

Board & MLS dues:

Due dates on my Board & MLS dues:

Broker fees:

Tech / software / online costs:

Cost for classes I need to take this year:

Other business expenses:

My fixed personal costs:

Living expenses:

Monthly credit card balances:

Other personal financial obligations:

My break-even point:

Do the math. Add your business and living expenses and see how many closings you need to make it all work, including setting aside 30% for taxes. (Tip: I'll help you with this in a couple pages.)

ADD: All sources of income (less broker split and less 30% taxes)

SUBTRACT: All expenses

BALANCE: What is left over?

REVENUE LIFECYCLE & REFERRALS

A REALTOR'S
REVENUE LIFECYCLE

1. CONVERSATION
2. LEAD
3. APPOINTMENT
4. HIRING
5. PREP
6. ACTIVE
7. OFFER
8. NEGOTIATION
9. CONTRACT
10. CLOSING
11. PAYCHECK
12. REFERRAL

The revenue life cycle diagram is designed to outline three things:

ONE. CONVERSATIONS

Everything in this business starts with a conversation. This is the lowest common denominator in generating more sales. Are you having enough conversations to meet your goals?

TWO. CONVERSION

Every step in the revenue life cycle involves a conversion to get to the next step. Each conversion typically involves knowing what to say. How are your conversion rates?

THREE. REFERRALS

Referrals start the life cycle all over again. Are you just asking for referrals at closing, or are you asking for referrals in every single step?

Discuss.

BASIC BUSINESS GOALS

Let's simplify your business with a little math by completing the following exercise:

EASY MATH. (Fill in the blanks, round up for partial numbers)

Amount of MONEY I need/want/intend to make this year:

A [ ]

My average home SALES PRICE is

B [ ]

My average COMMISSION is (B x 3% or 2.5%?)   **Bx3% = C** [ ]

To roughly adjust for broker split & taxes: **C x 60% = C*** [ ]

# of CLOSINGS PER YEAR: **A/C* = D** [ ]

# of CLOSINGS PER MONTH: **D/12 = E** [ ]

EASY MATH PAGE 2.

of CLOSINGS per month: E [ ]

# of APPOINTMENTS I need per month to hit my CLOSING goal: [ ]

# of LEADS I need per month to hit my APPOINTMENT goal: [ ]

# of CONVERSATIONS I need per month to hit my LEAD goal: [ ]

# of CONVERSATIONS per week (above / 4):   [ ]

# of CONVERSATIONS per DAY (above / 6):   [ ]

Notes & Variations:

- Your commission may be less than 3% so adjust as necessary
- Do this exercise twice … once for target goal, again for stretch goal
- Closings per month … always round up to the next number (you cannot close half a property).
- It all comes down to conversations. Are you having enough conversations to support your goals?
- See example on next page.

BASIC BUSINESS GOALS ... EXAMPLE!

EASY MATH.

Amount of MONEY I need/want/intend to make this year:	**A**	$100,000
My average home SALES PRICE is	**B**	$300,000
My average COMMISSION is (B x 3% or 2.5%?)	**Bx3% = C**	$9,000
To roughly adjust for broker split & taxes:	**C x 60% = C***	$5,400
# of CLOSINGS PER YEAR:	**A/C = D**	18.52 = 19
# of CLOSINGS PER MONTH:	**D/12 = E**	1.58 = 2

EASY MATH PAGE 2.

This example is an OVERGENERALIZATION and involves MANY ASSUMPTIONS. The source of your leads, the quality of your conversations, and your ability to consistently follow up will greatly impact your results. This exercise is designed to help you arrive at the understanding that the lowest common denominator in real estate sales success is simply the number of conversations you are having on a daily basis and setting that target to drive your success.

# of CLOSINGS I need per month to hit my income goal: E | 2 |

# of APPOINTMENTS I need per month to hit my CLOSING goal: | 8 |

# of LEADS I need per month to hit my APPOINTMENT goal: | 16 |

# of CONVERSATIONS I need per month to hit my LEAD goal: | 80 |

# of CONVERSATIONS per week (above / 4): | 20 |

# of CONVERSATIONS per DAY (above / 6): | 3.33 = 4 |

Let's walk through this a bit. In this example, I assumed that I needed:

- 4 appointments for every closing; so 1 out of every 4 appointments would result in a closing within a few months; 4 x 2 = 8;
- 2 leads to equal 1 appointment; so for every 2 solid leads I receive, I am able to set 1 appointment; 2 x 8 = 16;
- and that it takes me 5 conversations to equal 1 lead; 16 x 5 = 80;
- so that equals 20 conversations per week or 4 per day;
- if I consistently have 4 quality lead gen conversations per day, I'll hit my $100,000 income goal.

Your numbers will vary.

CONVERSATIONS

You are in the business of having conversations with people about real estate.
Want more business? Have more conversations.

MATH.

The number of quality lead generation conversations I had:

Yesterday:

The day before:

The day before that:

Last week:

My daily minimum or my daily target of lead gen conversations =

QUANTITY:

Am I having enough conversations to meet my goals?

01 — 02 — 03 — 04 — 05 — 06 — 07 — 08 — 09 — 10

| Super disconnect between my activities and goals. | My lead gen activity is somewhat reflective of my goals... let's just say we're dating. | My lead gen activity is in a committed long-term relationship w/ my goals. |

QUALITY.

I am direct with my conversations and asking for business.

01 — 02 — 03 — 04 — 05 — 06 — 07 — 08 — 09 — 10

| Asking for business makes me uncomfortable. | I am more of a soft sell. | I ask for business quickly, directly, often. |

Here's how I think I rate with natural & authentic in my sales-related conversations:

01 — 02 — 03 — 04 — 05 — 06 — 07 — 08 — 09 — 10

| I feel awkard & uncomfortable in most sales conversations. | This sales conversation thing is a bit of a learned behavior, but I got it. | Super authentic totally in my DNA. |

My comfort level in reaching out for client opportunities looks like this:

01 — 02 — 03 — 04 — 05 — 06 — 07 — 08 — 09 — 10

| Uncomfortable, knot in stomach, avoidance, | This sales conversation thing is a bit of a learned behavior, but I got it. | I love it |

My relationship with the phone looks like this:

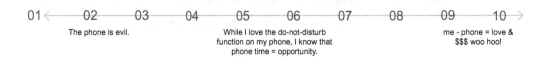

01 ← — 02 — 03 — 04 — 05 — 06 — 07 — 08 — 09 — 10 →

The phone is evil.

While I love the do-not-disturb
function on my phone, I know that
phone time = opportunity.

me - phone = love &
$$$ woo hoo!

Most of my communication is (rate them)…

Online   Email   Text   Phone   In person

THE POWER QUESTIONS

By now you understand that you are in the business of talking to people about real estate. But what do you say? When you realize that the majority of effective communication in this business (and in life, marriage, parenting, leading, and being a good friend) is simply asking good questions, it takes a lot of the pressure off and begins to put you in control of the conversation. It also puts you on the rapport fast-track. Just ask questions, powerful questions. Some questions are more strategic, more effective, than others. Let's take a look at a simple and authentic set of questions you can use in your business …

PQ #1: I wouldn't be doing my job
"Hey, real quick . . . I wouldn't be doing my job if I didn't ask you this question. Is there anyone you know who may need my services this year? I appreciate you keeping me in mind. I'll send you a quick email with my contact information. Are you anticipating any real estate needs this year?"

PQ #2: Earn your referrals
"I know you know a number of Realtors. I just want you to know that it is my goal to earn your referrals. Just planting the seed. So what's the most important thing that you value in a Realtor? While we're on the topic, are you guys anticipating any real estate needs this year?"

PQ #3: The second on your list
"I respect that you know another Realtor [or that your sister is a Realtor or that you like your old Realtor]. I'd love to be the second on your list. Not everyone is the right match, so keep me in mind. While we're on the topic, are you anticipating any real estate needs this year?"

PQ #4: The only property?
"Is this the only home you have to sell, or are there others?"

PQ #5: Who do you know?

"Who do you know who may need my services this year? We are already setting appointments for fall."

PQ #6: Mentioned real estate?

"Who do you know who has recently mentioned real estate?"

PQ #7: Who do you call?

"Who do you call when you have a real estate question?"

PQ WORKOUT SUGGESTIONS

You need some muscle memory around what to say and this typically involves spending some time with the material. Try some of these on for size:

- Pick one and write it out 20 times.

- Pick one and type it out 20 times.

- Pick one and rephrase it. How would I say this to my best friend or my mother?

- Record yourself on your cell phone (such as iphone Voice Memos) then play this recording in your car (hands-free, of course) for 30 days.

- Get a script partner and set an 8am phone appointment with each other M-F for four weeks in a row and recite these back and forth.

- Try these out on your spouse or bff and ask for their feedback.

- Walk around the house (by yourself) and say the PQ's outloud for 20 minutes 5 days in a row.

- Practice with a funny accent.

- Practice with the dog and see if you can get him to give you that funny head tilt thing that dogs do.

MY PEOPLE

Build your village; love on them.

MY 5 PEOPLE

Who are five people I know who know everyone?

1	2	3	4	5

Who are five people who would give me the shirt off their back, who believe in me, who would not hesitate to help me if I asked?

1	2	3	4	5

Who are five people I know who started their own business or have done something professionally impressive?

1	2	3	4	5

What is my top community involvement or local network, and who are my favorite five people in that network?

1	2	3	4	5

MY WORLD (groups) What groups am I connected to?

MY TOP 100 Who are my top 100 people anywhere?

MY ONLINE AUDIT

Your customers and potential customers are online and they will Google you (even your friends) before they call you. Let's see how you're showing up and improve your online presence.

MY ONLINE AUDIT. Where am I online? Is it accurate, current? Does it accurately portray me as a professional? When someone Googles me, what is their first impression?

- Google my name
- Google my name plus title, plus firm, plus town
- Google my email address, phone number, old email address, old phone number
- Do the same in Google Images
- Do this exercise on BOTH your computer and someone else's. Why? Because the cache on your hard drive remembers all your data and what websites you have clicked so it will be easier to research yourself on your computer than it will be on someone else's.
- Bonus exercise: Google a few of your favorite Realtors and see what websites they are on that perhaps you should consider.

WEBSITE LIST. What website profiles are important to me and my business and are they accurate with a current photo?

- My broker agent directory
- My local board
- LinkedIn
- Zillow
- Social Media
- Facebook "About Me" tab
- Others:

MY ACTION PLAN

Actions and scripts are where you do the heavy lifting of gaining clients faster.

WHY 24-HOUR ACTION IS SO IMPORTANT. Your brain needs help processing information. Your brain is always actively searching for the right information or experience to fill the gaps. 24-hour action sets things in motion. Adopt this habit with anything important.

My Aha	My 24-hour Action

ACTION ITEMS & SCRIPT REFERENCE

Whether launching or relaunching, action is everything. Success Faster is less of a pep talk and more of a roadmap, a to-do guide for gaining momentum. If you engage in the action -- really, truly do the work -- I would bank on your success. The more time you spend on mastering what to say, the greater your conversions will be in the revenue life cycle.

A note on scripts: Yes, tweak as necessary. Always tweak the scripts so they sound and feel natural for you. Always strive for authentic. And then practice. Practice until it becomes your habitual language. Owning the language of real estate will do amazing things for your confidence and swagger, and will put money in the bank.

ACTION ITEM. Call Your Mother

Call your mother. Seriously, call your mother (or your sister or bff), and here's what you are going to say:

> *"Mom (sister, bff), I just started at [broker name] today! OMG, I am so excited! Wish I had done this earlier. I need your help. This is day one of the training program and the very first assignment they gave me was to call you! This business is seriously referral-based, and I have big goals. Will you help me? It's now my job to know the real estate needs of my friends and family and their friends and families, so there is a basic question, actually two questions, that I need to ask you. 1. Are you anticipating any real estate needs this year? 2. Is there anyone you know who may need my services this year? It's pretty much my job to ask this question, and who better to start with than you? I really super appreciate your support."*

ACTION ITEM: Identifying Your TOP 100

Get out your phone. Get your neighborhood list. Your church directory. Your Christmas card list. Your kids' school directory. Your former colleagues. Your golf league. Don't forget your family. In town or out of town or out of state…all of them. Your college friends. I have brand-new agents who got their first or second client because they called their cousin or college friend halfway across the country. You know a LOT of people! Let's identify your top 100, because I promise you, there is business in there. Your immediate job is to cultivate and coax the leads out of that top 100 list.

ACTION ITEM: TOP 100, Calling

Call one to twenty of your TOP 100, and here's what to say:

> *"Hey, Sam, it's [me]. Do you have a minute? I know you're at work, so I'll be fast. I wanted to let you know what I'm doing. I've thought about this for years, finally pulled the trigger, and I am now an associate with xyz Realty. Love it! Wish I had done this sooner! So a couple of quick questions: 1. Do you have a go-to Realtor when you have a real estate question? [NO: Great, you do now! Or YES: Great, happy to be the second person on your list.] Second question: Are you anticipating any real estate needs this year or know anyone who may need my services? I appreciate you keeping me in mind. I'll send you an email right away so you have my contact info. Everything good with you? Would love to do lunch or happy hour sometime, catch up. What's your schedule like the next couple of weeks?"*

ACTION ITEM: Affordability Factor

You're talking to renters. Quickly, make a list of everyone you know who rents or probably has a lot of friends or colleagues who rent. If there is an employer in your town who hires a lot of millennials, figure out who you know who works there. I am in Austin, Texas, so this topic is a great tool for my 20-something and 30-something friends who work at tech start-ups downtown, or who work at Google, or Facebook, or Apple. One way or another, figure out how to have this conversation with as many renters as possible:

"Oh, you're renting? Have you thought about buying? You know, interest rates are historically low. Like they'll never be lower. They will go up . . . not if, but when. Well, I thought of you this morning because I was thinking of this. Have you thought of buying? If you did buy, what neighborhood interests you?

"Your timing can be critical because when interest rates go up, let's say from 4% to 5% that will impact how much home you could buy. If you qualified for that cute $250,000 home in Shady Grove today, you may only qualify for a $230,000 home next year. And prices are going up. I'd hate to see you miss the market, miss the opportunity to live in Shady Grove. Does this topic interest you? I thought so.

Would you like to meet for coffee to talk about it more, or I can introduce you to a mortgage broker just to explore your options . . . which sounds better? Is there anyone else you know who is renting who should probably take a look at this?

"Hey, while we're on the topic, is there anyone you know who may need my services this year? We're already setting up appointments for this summer. Keep me in mind . . . I'd love the opportunity to help your friends and colleagues. I'm going to shoot you an email real quick so you have my info handy."

ACTION ITEM: Mondays!

Here's what to say to anyone with whom you've had a real estate conversation over the past few days or on the weekend:

"As I said I would, I just wanted to follow up on our real estate conversation from Saturday. Is this an OK time? Great. So tell me again what you're thinking, what your needs are. [Listen. Ask questions.]"

Then set a timeframe for your next follow-up and email something of value [maybe just a follow-up email to recap the conversation, or possibly an article on the topic or a personal note]. Make a note in your calendar [or whatever system you're using, your

CRM] for the follow-up. Then ask this question (the POWER QUESTION which we will scuba dive into in the next chapter):

> *"Hey, real quick, while we're on the topic… Is there anyone else you know who may need my services this year? We're already setting up appointments for [summer] and I always want to make sure I am saving spots for my friends and their friends. Thank you for thinking about it. My business is primarily referral-based and I appreciate your support."*

ACTION ITEM: CRM

Take 30 minutes and do a Google search for best Realtor CRMs. Read a couple reviews comparing them. Maybe ask your Realtor network what CRM they are using and what they like best about it. The other option is take 30 minutes and go over a couple tutorials or best-practices articles on the CRM you are already using, or is made available to you.

ACTION ITEM: Power Questions (PQs)

Read the PQs again and the how's-the-market responses out loud ten times fast. Another option is to pair up with another agent and plow through this exercise together. The goal of this quick exercise is simply speed and repetition. Speed and repetition. In fact, you may want to do this simple exercise every day this week and next week and the week after. Go over and over and over and over these questions. Speak them out loud, write them out on a notepad, type them out, record yourself on your phone, and listen to them in your car (hands-free, of course). Speed and repetition.

The call: Pick one of the PQs in this chapter and call someone, call five, call twenty… heck, walk your block and ask your neighbors. This is not an email, it is not a post on Facebook. You must have conversations with people. Do not move on to the next action without this ACTION ITEM checked off.

ACTION ITEM: Start Your Bio Document

Start a fresh new document on your laptop, name it BIO. Keep this simple because you can build on it later. Write out three basics:

1. List of credentials
2. Short bio, 2-3 sentences
3. Medium bio including a personal sentence.

Tip: search your agent directory or LinkedIn or Zillow for examples of well-written bio's.

ACTION ITEM: Call Your Biggest Advocate, Again

Sometimes our closest people can be our biggest advocates and our biggest critics. So the conversation may be as simple as giving that important person an update on how you're doing. It may look something like this:

> *"Hi. It's me. I wanted to give you a little report of how things are going at work. I want you to see how serious I am and tell you a couple things I have going on. Got a minute?*
>
> *"First, I really appreciate your support. So I [then go on to tell them about your open houses, the buyer you're working with, that as the national sales manager of your real estate business you basically go to the office in the morning and do not leave until you have talked with x number of people about real estate . . . or some pertinent fact about what you're doing]."*

Then ask if you can practice a script or two with them over the phone.

> *"So I spend about an hour a day just practicing what to say, my presentations, and studying the market. I realized I would like a little real feedback, trying to get this to sound natural. I want to run this by you, get your feedback."*

Then practice with them. They may laugh a little; they usually offer a little advice like "be yourself," then half the time they'll mention someone who may have a real estate need. You always want to end with a question, something like this:

"Is there anyone you have come across recently who mentioned real estate?"

And then you need to train them HOW to help you:

"When you do hear of someone, don't just give them my card. Instead, say this: "You know what? I really want to introduce you to/have you talk to my friend [your name]. She's the friend I mentioned who is a Realtor. What's your email? I'm just going to send an email that introduces the two of you. No pressure; she'll treat you like family and may be able to help you. At the very least, she'll be a good resource."

ACTION ITEM: Find Your Five People

Your top five people, get them on the phone. Here's what to say:

"I promised myself I would call you today. Do you have a second?

Option 1: *"You know everyone. You probably know more people than anyone I know. That's why I'm calling. I have big goals for my business this year. Here's my quick and easy question: Who do you know that I should know?"*

Option 2: *"You love me, right? I need your help. I have big goals for my business this year. Here's my quick and easy question: Who do you know that I should know?"*

Option 3: *"You've started your own business/ you've accomplished some impressive things. That's why I'm calling. I have big goals for my business this year. Come have coffee with me. I want to ask you about your success, advice for starting something new. I figure I should listen to successful people and you're on my shortlist. What is your availability this week or next?"*

Option 4: *"How can I help you? You have always been very supportive of me and my business. How can I help you? How is your business? What are you working on? Is there anyone I know that you would like to meet? Let's have coffee and catch up."*

ACTION ITEM: Local Businesses

Pop in to ten local businesses and introduce yourself. This can be especially helpful when it is an area of town that you regularly visit or that you live in or near. Are you in a smaller town? Then stop by every single business. Focus on whatever it takes to get into conversations with people. And keep going back. Start building that recognition of you as Realtor, you as hard-working Realtor. Sometimes it is as simple as a "Hello, it's your favorite Realtor again!" What if you started meeting all your favorite people and connections in the same coffee shop all the time and you got to know the coffee shop owner and the staff? Back to the pop-ins at the local businesses. Here's what to say:

> *"I live nearby, and I realized I did not know every small business in the neighborhood, so I thought I'd drop by and introduce myself. I am a Realtor who specializes in this area of town.*
>
> *Where do you live? Do you have a go-to Realtor? When you have a real estate question, who do you call? Do you have any real estate needs this year or know someone who could use my services?*
>
> *Here's my card in case you hear of someone. Do you have a card? I appreciate your time. I'll stop by again. I like this place. What's the one thing I should know about your business? [listen] Great. I am going to send some business your way. Have a great day."*

And note, you may want to buy something while you're there, if appropriate. That may work best for the coffee shop or gift store or auto parts store, not so much for the car dealership. But speaking of car dealerships, when I bought my Mini Cooper in 2010, my sales guy, Charlie, turned into a client. And then go back and go back and go back. And send a friend or two or three in there and make sure they mention you with some form of, "My good friend Susan the Realtor sent me."

ACTION ITEM: Find Your Favorite

Review all the ACTION ITEMS in each chapter (and there is an ACTION ITEM reference section near the end of the book). What did you like? Identify one ACTION ITEM that you really enjoyed. And then double down on this. Whatever you enjoyed the most will most likely produce the most opportunity. If all of your leads are coming from friends, then call friends today with this: "Hey, it's [me]. Got a minute? I realized all my business so far has come from friends or their friends. It's the thing I like most about the business. In order to hit my goals this month, I need two appointments every week. Who do you know I should talk to?" If you have had FSBO luck so far or you just like talking to for-sale-by-owners, try this:

> *"Hey, Mr. FSBO. It's John with ABC Realty. I specialize in helping FSBOs get their homes sold, so I wanted to check in and see how it's going, see if you have any questions. Can you tell me a bit about the home? Are you familiar with the two required disclosures for sellers? At what point do you think you'll consider hiring a Realtor for the job of selling your home? I have a sign in my car right now. We could have the home on the market in no time."*

ACTION ITEM: Identify Your Procrastination

What did you miss? Identify one ACTION ITEM from the book that you either did not do (for whatever reason) or fell short on. Is there something you have said you would do, but it remains untouched? Sometimes it is just a matter of building more skill in that particular area and then results start to show up. Run with one of the items you have been avoiding and get more conversations under your belt.

ACTION ITEM: Your Calendar

- Block one hour every day Monday through Friday and call it "practice."
- Set a recurring appointment with at least two of these daily practice appointments where you are practicing with another agent.
- Set a recurring appointment for every day M-F, first thing in the morning, and call it "pipeline building." Your task with this daily focus is lead gen and to ask yourself the question "What is my fastest route to a lead, client or contract today?" (At the end of the day, ask yourself this question: Did I add to my pipeline today?)
- Tell someone about this plan, this task, this goal. Someone in your household works nicely or a good friend or family member or your broker. Tell them that you are telling them so that they'll help you stay accountable.
- Print out a two-month calendar and post it on the wall somewhere. For every day that you hit your appointment, highlight the day.

ACTION ITEM: Your Vision … Write It Down

Dr. Gail Matthews, a psychology professor at the Dominican University, found that the likelihood of hitting your goals increases a whopping 42% if you write them down. So let's do that.

What success looks like to me:

My financial goals are

My personal goals are

My five-year vacation plan is

Here's how I will change the world:

My sacred mission is

BOOK CLUB GROUP DISCUSSION GUIDE

Regular masterminding with colleagues and peers -- whether online or in person, in the cloud, zoom.com, in your living room, a conference room, or coffee shop -- gather your professional tribe. Use this guide to promote valuable conversation and thought around how you're showing up, what you do well, what you are focused on, where you are going, and how to get there. Together, we are better.

Sexy Real Estate: Some of the cool reasons I got into real estate in the first place are … or here is what appealed to me the most or was most exciting to me … or my greatest motivation when I first got started was …

Super Powers: My special super powers are (toddler wrangling, opportunity magnet, client whisperer, mad phone skills, ability to read between the lines) …

Story: My favorite client experience ever is this …

Success: Here is how I would summarize my business success so far …

Vision: Here is my business success vision …

Quickly: Fast beats smart, hustle matters, clients faster … discuss.

Pivot Record: My career pivot record looks like this …

Pivot2: What minor pivots, maybe a course correction, do I need to make in my business?

Pivot3: Am I due for a major pivot?

School: I wish they would have told me this in school …

Rookie Advice: My advice to someone just getting started is this …

Take 2: If I were to start my business over, here is what I would do different …

NSM: I am the National Sales Manager of my business. How am I doing?

Fav: My favorite go-to lead generation script looks like this …

Direct: I am direct in asking for business. Discuss.

5: My 5 people are …

Ease: The easiest thing for me in my business is …

Procrastinate: I tend to procrastinate this in my business …

Magic Wand: If I could wave a magic wand over my business, here is what I would create …

Fix: If I could fix one thing in my business today, I would fix …

Vacation: Here is how you take time off in this business …

Accountability: I could use a little more accountability in this area …

24-hour: Based on our discussions today, my 24-hour action item is ...

ONLINE RESOURCES

Find the book on Amazon

www.successfasterbook.com
Available in paperback, Kindle, Audible

Join the 456 Coaching Club Facebook group

www.facebook.com/groups/456club
Join other agents engaged in the Success Faster conversation.

Follow

Follow Julie Nelson and The Nelson Project and the 456 Coaching Club for future updates to this guide as well as best practices for new and emerging REALTORS®. If it is social and media, chances are you'll find me by searching The Nelson Project or thenelsonproject; in the case of Twitter, follow @julienelsonATX.

Julie's Austin, Texas Real Estate Business

www.thenelsonproject.com

Julie's Coaching And Training Blog

www.thenelsonproject.org

NOTE PAGES
for you and your book club!

NOTE PAGES
for you and your book club!

_____

_____

_____

_____

_____

_____

_____

_____

_____

_____

_____

_____

_____

_____

_____

_____

_____

_____

_____

_____

_____

NOTE PAGES
for you and your book club!

NOTE PAGES
for you and your book club!

NOTE PAGES

for you and your book club!

Printed in the USA
CPSIA information can be obtained
at www.ICGtesting.com
LVHW081136120324
774259LV00025B/464